DATE DUE

Ancient West African Kingdoms:
Ghana, Mali, & Songhai

MARY QUIGLEY

Heinemann Library
Chicago, Illinois

© 2002 Reed Educational & Professional Publishing
Published by Heinemann Library,
an imprint of Reed Educational & Professional Publishing,
Chicago, Illinois

Customer service: 888-454-2279

Visit our website at www.heinemannlibrary.com

Design and map illustrations by Depke Design
Printed and bound in the United States by Lake Book Manufacturing, Inc.

06 05 04 03 02
10 9 8 7 6 5 4 3 2 1

Library of Congress Cataloging-in-Publication Data
Quigley, Mary, 1963-
    Ancient West African kingdoms : Ghana, Mali, and Songhai / Mary Quigley.
        p. cm. -- (Understanding people in the past)
    Includes bibliographical references and index.
    Summary: Examines the social, economic, political, and cultural life of the people of ancient Ghana, Mali, and Songhai, including profiles of influential citizens.
    ISBN 1-58810-425-7 (HC), 1-4034-0098-9 (Pbk.)
    1. Mali (Empire)--Juvenile literature. 2. Ghana (Empire)--Juvenile literature. 3. Songhai Empire--Juvenile literature. 4. Africa, West--History--Juvenile literature. [1. Mali (Empire) 2. Ghana (Empire) 3. Songhai Empire. 4. Africa, West--History.]   I. Title. II. Series.
    DT532.2 .Q85 2002
    966'.01--dc21
                            2001005327

Acknowledgments
The author and publisher are grateful to the following for permission to reproduce copyright material:

Cover photograph © 2002 Wolfgang Kaehler

Title page, pp. 9, 43 Carol Beckwith/Angela Fisher/Robert Estall Photo Library; pp. 5, 6T, 10, 12T, 15, 22, 25, 26T, 27, 31, 33, 37, 39T, 39B, 40, 41T, 42, 48, 49, 52, 59 © 2002 Wolfgang Kaehler; p. 6B Jacques Jangoux/Photo Researcher, Inc.; p. 7T Art Wolfe/Photo Researcher, Inc.; p.7B Douglas Waugh/Peter Arnold, Inc.; pp. 8, 21, 28, 29, 46B, 58 M.&A. Kirtley/ANA Agence; p.11, 46T Werner Forman Archive/Art Resource, NY; p. 13 Ghana National Museum, Accra/Art Resource, NY; p. 17 Franko Khoury/National Museum of African Art, Smithsonian Institution; p. 18 Erich Lessing/Art Resource, NY; p. 19 Giraudon/Art Resource, NY; p. 23 Ferdinando Scianna/Magnum Photos; pp. 24T, 36 Mary Evans Picture Library; p. 24B Abbas/Magnum Photos; p. 26B Lineair/Peter Arnold, Inc.; pp. 30T, 51 The Newark Museum/Art Resource; p. 30B Bruno Barbey/Magnum Photos; p. 32 Carol Beckwith/ Robert Estall Photo Library; p. 34 Hans Pfletschinger/Peter Arnold, Inc.; p. 35 M.&A. Kirtley; p. 38 Martha Cooper/Peter Arnold, Inc.; p. 41B Lineair (R. Gling)/Peter Arnold, Inc.; p. 44 M&E Bernheim/Woodfin Camp & Associates; p. 45 Phil Borden/Photo Edit, Inc.; p. 46T Werner Forman/Art Resource, NY; pp. 47, 55 George Gerster/Photo Researchers, Inc; p. 50 Chris Hellier/Corbis; p. 53 Victor Englebert/Photo Researchers, Inc.; p. 56 Mansell/TimePix; p. 57 Werner Forman Archive/Musaum fur Volkerkunde, Berlin/Art Resource.

Every effort has been made to contact copyright holders of any material reproduced in this book. Any omissions will be rectified in subsequent printings if notice is given to the publisher.

Some words are shown in bold, **like this.** You can find out what they mean by looking in the glossary.

Contents

Who Were the Ancient West Africans?

A hidden land

West Africa is the region of Africa on the Atlantic Coast, between the **Sahara** to the north and rain forest to the south. Because the Sahara is difficult to cross, West Africa remained unknown to the world for a very long time.

For centuries, Europeans heard tales of a land of gold in Africa. But no one could say exactly where the West African kingdoms were. For a long time West Africa was called *terra incognita,* which means "unknown land."

West Africa was difficult to explore. The Sahara is a large, sandy barrier for travelers and there were many insects and diseases in the area.

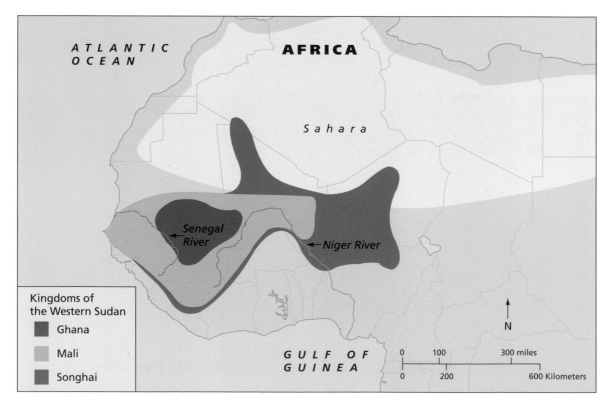

ATLANTIC OCEAN

AFRICA

Sahara

Senegal River

← Niger River

Kingdoms of the Western Sudan
- Ghana
- Mali
- Songhai

GULF OF GUINEA

N

0   100   300 miles

0   200   600 Kilometers

Africans formed groups that sometimes became very powerful, and so their territory grew larger. Because of a powerful group's influence, their territory sometimes became a kingdom.

In West Africa, three famous kingdoms were created during ancient times: Ghana, Mali, and Songhai. Ghana lasted from around 700 C.E. until 1076. Mali lasted from the 1100s to the late 1400s. Songhai lasted from 1468 to 1591. These kingdoms had great achievements in art, religion, science, education, **trade,** government, and warfare. They also had rulers who are still known today. As one kingdom declined, another rose to take its place. Sometimes this transition took many years.

West Africans come from many different clans and groups. Thousands of languages and dialects are spoken throughout the area.

5

Gift of the Niger River

West Africa is hot and sandy in the north. Dust storms are common in the dry regions. The middle region is affected by the flood cycles of the Niger River. The Niger River provides water for people, animals, and plants. The south is a grassland.

Sahel is the **Arabic** word for shore. It is often used to name the areas where the ancient kingdoms of Ghana, Mali, and Songhai were. The **Sahara** can be thought of as an ocean of sand, and the kingdoms that bordered the Sahara were on its "shore."

Animals

The variety of animals in West Africa today are similar to the animals found during ancient times. Giraffes, lions, elephants, and crocodiles live there. Hippopotamuses can still be seen escaping the heat in waterways. Dolphins and manatees swim along the coast. Monkeys and other **primates** play in the branches of trees. West Africa is also known for its variety of birds.

Plants

The baobab tree is a familiar sight in Africa. It can grow to be very large and looks like it has roots for branches. People collect

The Sahara is an ocean of sand. Sometimes blinding dust storms can occur, making travel difficult.

Not all of West Africa is sandy and dry. There are **fertile** areas along the rivers and rain forests.

Monkeys and other primates are common in West Africa. They can be found playing in the branches of trees.

rainwater from the hollow of its trunk, and many kinds of animals make their homes in it. The leaves are made into sauces for food and are also used for healing wounds. The pods, sometimes called monkey bread, contain seeds that can be eaten or made into a drink. West Africans sometimes use the empty pods as cups and bowls.

Plants become more abundant farther south of the Sahara. The landscape changes from scrub bushes to grasses and grains. Even farther south in the rain forest, plantains and kola nuts grow.

West Africans have discovered that the baobab tree has many beneficial uses.

How Do We Know About the Ancient West Africans?

We have learned much about West Africa from the accounts of **traders** who took stories back to other regions.

Ibn Battuta

Ibn Battuta was a famous **Arab** who wrote down his travels, providing information about ancient West Africa. Ibn Battuta visited Mali during the reign of **Mansa** Suleyman in the mid 1300s. He wrote about the fairness of the West Africans and how they could not stand any injustice. According to Ibn Battuta, food was plentiful and inexpensive in Mali.

A lot of West African history is hidden in the earth. Erosion and **archaeologists** help to uncover West African **artifacts**.

Oral traditions

Even before visitors came to West Africa, the oral tradition ensured that history was remembered and passed along to each new generation. Storytellers, called **griots,** knew and retold the important stories of the West African people.

Finding ancient treasure

Archaeologists have made discoveries that add to our understanding of ancient West Africa. They have found pottery, weapons, jewelry, and other artifacts when soil is eroded or when they **excavate.**

In 1914, archaeologists found the **ruins** of the Ghana capital of Kumbi Saleh. In two large mansions they found finely made weapons, farming tools, glass weights for weighing gold, and fragments of pottery. In the city of Jenne, archaeologists have found beads and the foundation of a round house.

Archaeologists use artifacts and other resources, such as Ibn Battuta's writings, to piece together a picture of West African life. They have been able to find out much about West African religion, technology, economy, and art.

This **fertility** figure is just one of the objects that archaeologists have used to piece together life in ancient West Africa.

9

History in Pictures and Words

One of the many things that **archaeologists** are interested in are the pictures left behind by past civilizations. West Africans made pictures on stone walls and pottery. Their pictures were often geometric, with shapes of animals and other things that were part of their daily life and religious beliefs.

Ancient West Africans also left behind many pieces of art, such as sculptures and metalwork.

Pictures on useful objects, such as these lidded jars, were not only beautiful to the people of West Africa, but also meaningful.

Griots

The modern tradition of **griots** has kept the West African past alive. Within the griots' tales are the rise and fall of empires, the life stories of famous people, traditional family values, religious beliefs, and social rules.

Written records

In addition to a strong oral tradition, some written records of ancient West Africa exist. The *Epic of Sundiata* is a well-known story that has been passed along by griots. It has also been translated and written down. Travelers like Ibn Battuta wrote about Africa. Volumes of manuscripts in **Arabic** show the effect of **Islam** upon West Africa.

> **The *Epic of Sundiata***
> The *Epic of Sundiata* is a story about Sundiata Keita, the Lion King. It is a famous story that tells of how Sundiata overcame a physical disability and his enemies to become a great king. Many people tell this story, though they always add extra details depending on the audience.

When Islam spread to West Africa, people needed to be able to read the **Qur'an.** This caused a new interest in learning to read and write among West Africans.

Ghana

The empire of Ghana began around 300 C.E. in a region known as *Bilad es Sudan* or "land of the blacks." Today, this region is still referred to as the Sudan. The state of Wagadu was founded by the Soninke people on an **oasis** along an important **trade** route.

Wagadu becomes Ghana

It is said that in about 700 C.E., a great warrior and **diplomat** from the royal **clan** Ouagadou unified the Soninke people and formed a kingdom. The chief was known as the *kaya maghan* or "king of the gold." He was also known as *ghana,* which means "war chief" in the Mande language. The state of Wagadu eventually grew into the empire of Ghana.

Ghana was founded on an oasis by the Soninke people. The oasis was a favorite place for travelers and traders to stop after crossing the **Sahara.**

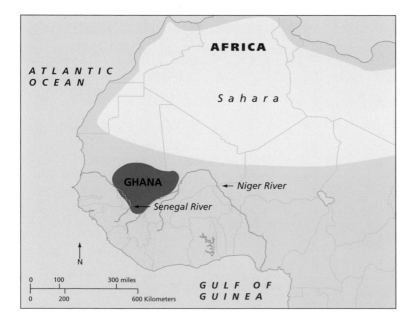

This map shows the ancient kingdom of Ghana, which lasted from around 700 to 1076.

Iron weapons

The Soninke people made their weapons out of iron. Neighboring peoples still made their weapons out of stone, wood, and bone. Their weapons were no match against the iron weapons of the Soninke people.

Trade and wealth

Ghana also benefited from being located between the Niger and Senegal Rivers. People from around the region had to travel the rivers to trade.

Gold made Ghana wealthy even though the people of Ghana did not mine any themselves. The gold was in a region south of Ghana. Traders who came through Ghana to spend or buy gold were charged taxes upon entry and on their way out. Ghana became wealthy from collecting these taxes.

In 1076 C.E., Ghana lost a war—called a **jihad**—with **Muslims.** Out of this time of disorder came an opportunity for the emergence of another kingdom, Mali.

The people of Ghana made weapons with iron; these new, stronger weapons helped Ghana defeat enemies.

Mali emerged as the next great West African kingdom after Ghana. The Mali empire lasted from the early twelfth century until the middle of the fifteenth century. Mali grew out of a state named Kangaba, far south in the original kingdom of Ghana.

Before Mali emerged as a great empire, it is believed that the **Mandinka** people of this region were journeying to the gold regions along the Senegal River and transporting the gold to Ghana for **trade.** The Senegal and Niger Rivers made Mali a **fertile** area with "highways" of water. The Mandinka people were farmers who **cultivated** rice and other valuable crops. They were also expert **traders.** Their great success in farming and trade and their control of the rivers increased their power in West Africa.

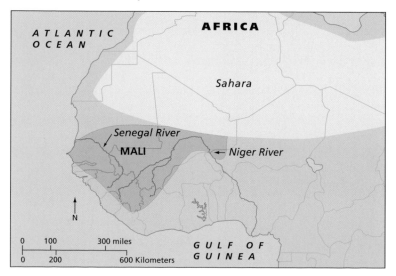

Mali became an even larger kingdom than Ghana. According to a fourteenth-century Egyptian historian, Al Omari, it took four months to travel across it by donkey or camel.

From state to kingdom

Under the leadership of Sundiata Keita, the kingdom of Mali formed. **Griots** still sing the epic story of Sundiata, the Lion King of Mali. The name Mali means "where the king resides." The kings of Mali were **Muslims.** The religion of **Islam** brought much **cultural** exchange between West Africa and the Middle East.

After Sundiata, the kings of Mali took the title **mansa,** which means "lord" in the Mandinka language.

This woman is dressed as the people of ancient Mali dressed hundreds of years ago.

Sundiata Keita

Sundiata Keita was the son of a king. He was his father's choice to take over the kingdom. When Sundiata was young, he could not walk and rarely spoke. Many doubted that he could ever be a king. When his father was dying, he arranged for Sundiata to have a **griot**. Sundiata's griot was the son of the king's griot. Since griots were so important during that time, this showed others that the king wanted Sundiata to inherit the throne.

Sundiata's mother was protective of her son. He grew strong and tried to make her proud. Eventually he was so strong that no one else could draw his bow. When his half-brother claimed the throne, Sundiata's mother took her son into **exile** for his safety.

Return from exile

Sundiata later returned to Mali, after an unpopular leader named Sumanguru had taken over. Sundiata **liberated** the **Mandinka** people with the help of his griot. Sundiata's griot used a **balaphon** to charm their enemies.

There is a story that has been handed down about Sundiata's victory. In the story, Sumanguru's army appeared on the horizon in the shape of a cloud and Sundiata's army

This statue shows Sundiata Keita on horseback. He overcame physical challenges to become a strong leader.

took the form of a mountain. Sundiata defeated Sumanguru with an arrow tipped with the poisoned nail of a rooster. Sundiata then became known as the Lion King.

The Lion King

Sundiata was loved by his subjects. He was known throughout Mali for his kindness, intelligence, and ability to settle disputes. Sundiata believed in **cultural** exchange. He sent his children to study in other regions. He thought that children who were friends in their youth would not be enemies in adulthood.

Mansa Musa

Another famous leader of Mali was Kankan Musa, later known as **Mansa** Musa. He was a **Muslim** and relative of Sundiata Keita. He wanted Mali to be **Islamic,** but mansas did not force others to adopt certain beliefs. Islam and traditional West African religions were practiced side by side in the same communities. Sometimes people even practiced both religions.

In 1324, Mansa Musa made a **pilgrimage** to **Mecca,** in modern western Saudi Arabia, the city where Islam was started. All Muslims consider it very important that they make a trip to Mecca. For Mansa Musa, that meant a year of travel. It has been estimated that more than 15,000 people may have traveled with Mansa Musa to Mecca. They were seen carrying staffs of gold. Mansa Musa gave away so much gold when he passed through Cairo that its economy was affected for more than twenty years. Mansa Musa's pilgrimage made an impression on the world. Mali began to appear on maps throughout the Middle East and Europe.

Mansa Musa traveled to the Muslim holy city of Mecca with a huge caravan. It would have looked similar to this picture.

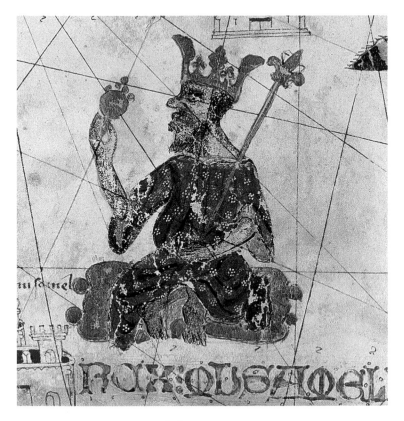

The travels of Mansa Musa, pictured here, made faraway nations aware of the **culture** of West Africa.

Mansa Musa's achievements

Mansa Musa expanded the borders of Mali in all directions. He created more **trade** routes, and the cities of Gao and Timbuktu emerged. He brought architects to Mali to design **mosques** and introduced West Africans to brick houses with flat roofs.

He established schools and law courts. Reading and writing began to flourish. Mansa Musa impressed leaders from other places because of all the things he had done. He brought much attention to Mali.

Songhai's rise

In 1325, **Mansa** Musa's soldiers captured two princes from the city of Gao. Since the princes were the children of kings, they were treated well. Prince Ali Kolon became a valued soldier who led military expeditions for Mansa Musa. The princes missed their home, though, and wished to return someday.

Ali Kolon took military assignments closer and closer to Gao. He stored weapons and supplies along the way in case he ever had an opportunity to escape. After Mansa Musa died, the princes fled to Gao. They found that their father had died and a new king had taken over. They overthrew the new king and declared Gao independent. Gao and the Songhai people began to dominate the region that was once ruled by Ghana and Mali.

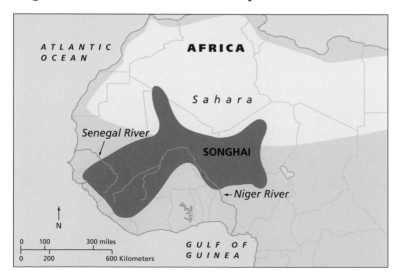

At its peak, Songhai was three times the size of Mali.

In addition to Gao and Timbuktu, the city of Jenne played a key role in the success of the Songhai empire. Jenne served as a link between the **traders** of Timbuktu and the gold miners in the south. Great blocks of salt were transported from Timbuktu to Jenne on canoes.

Songhai's fall

The kingdom of Songhai declined after an invasion by Morocco. The Moroccans beat the powerful armies of Songhai because they had a European weapon called a **harquebus.** They also had more troops.

Morocco never gained complete control of the Songhai territories. Natural disasters, raids, and the European slave trade furthered the decline of the Songhai empire.

The city of Jenne was key to the success of the Songhai empire. It formed a link between **trading** centers.

23

Sunni Ali

Sunni Ali was a military leader. He led the expansion of the Songhai empire. Sunni means "king." Sunni Ali respected the beliefs of the **Muslims** with whom his empire **traded,** but he did not forget the traditional ways. He knew that the farmers and fishermen who would be in his army still maintained their traditional beliefs.

Sunni Ali developed new methods of farming. He organized the boatmen of the Niger River into the beginnings of a professional navy.

The people who travel along the Niger River today still use the same type of boats and oars that the boatmen in Sunni Ali's time did.

Sunni Ali's son, Sunni Baru, became king when his father died in 1492. He was not a strict Muslim. Public ceremonies blended traditional and **Islamic** religious practice.

Askia Muhammed

Muhammed Turé, a devout Muslim, led a military **coup** and took over the Songhai government from Sunni Baru. After this, Muhammed Turé became known as **Askia** Muhammed. Askia Muhammed created a standing army. Now, the kingdom would not have to rely on volunteers pulled together on short notice. Because of the Muslim principle of equality, Askia Muhammed made sure that anyone— regardless of their **clan** membership—could advance in the government based on their own acheivements.

Askia Muhammed sought to make the cities, rather than the country, his base of support. Like **Mansa** Musa, he made a **pilgrimage** to **Mecca.** He is remembered for his political genius, religious beliefs, and military leadership.

Askia Muhammed emphasized the development of cities. This beautifully carved door can be found at Timbuktu.

23

Government

The system of government in ancient West Africa became more complex with each new kingdom.

Ghana

Princes were assigned to oversee provinces but were under the authority of the king. The king of Ghana was considered the father of all the Soninke people. He was also their religious leader, chief of their army, highest judge, and leader of the empire.

The government of Ghana used messengers on horseback to maintain communication with outlying regions.

Mali

Mansa Musa brought scholars from Egypt to Mali who set up schools and courts of law. The courts of law applied the values of the **Qur'an** to everyday life.

According to **Islam,** individuals were held accountable for their actions. **Muslim** courts of law were created. **Qadis** were Muslim judges.

Mansa Musa appointed governors to rule Mali's various provinces. He also had a group of advisers who regulated such things as fishing in the Niger River, traveling through Mali's forests, agriculture, and finance.

Songhai

By the time the Songhai empire was at its peak, the rulers needed a staff of advisers to oversee various regions and functions. The military was elaborately designed. **Askia** Muhammed created a structure of **officials** and sub-officials.

Traditional laws

Traditional African law made a family or **clan** accountable for any crimes committed by individual members. West Africans used good deeds and gifts, rather than physical punishment, to settle disputes. For a victim's family, this penalty helped them meet their survival needs if they lost the head of the family.

Traditional markets are still found in West African today. These markets usually follow traditional laws.

25

West African Clothing

Because of the warm climate of West Africa, people often wore little clothing. Clothing was sometimes used as protection from the heat. Fabric was worn to cover the face during dust and sand storms.

Women made slings with their clothes for carrying babies. This was comfortable for the babies. It was also convenient for mothers who were busy with chores or other tasks and needed their hands free.

This West African man is wearing a scarf to shield his face from dust and sand storms.

As in ancient times, West African women still modify their clothing to make it easier for them to care for their children.

Clothing for special occasions

Special clothing was worn for social or ceremonial reasons. Clothing could indicate social rank. During the Songhai time, the women of Timbuktu dressed luxuriously. During that time period the empire was very rich and prosperous. Thus, it showed in the clothes people wore. Men and women were fond of jewels. Women sometimes decorated their hair with bands of gold.

Clothes were generally made of materials that were readily available, such as woven plant fibers or materials from animals. **Trade** created more variety in clothing and types of weaving.

Sometimes special clothing was worn to show social status or for religious ceremonies.

Children

In West Africa, children were prized. A woman's **fertility** was valued. Art and music reflected a strong appreciation for children. The birth of a child was always celebrated with feasting, dancing, and singing. Sometimes men had several wives in order to have more children. Wealth was measured in terms of how large a family was. Children who lost parents were raised by relatives.

Children were treasured by West Africans. Having children was both a responsibility and a blessing.

Family groups were large and included a man and his wife or wives, children, and many relatives, both close and distant. All men were fathers, all women were mothers, and all children were sisters and brothers.

Clans

Villages were made of **clans.** Clans were headed by the oldest male member. Many clans had certain occupations that were passed along from generation to generation. Some clans specialized in metalwork. Others hunted or fished. Still other clans provided kings and the leaders of provinces.

Ancestors

West Africans did not forget their ancestors. They considered their ancestors to be an important part of their family. The living believed that they honored their ancestors by being decent human beings. They believed that if they were not decent human beings, their ancestors would punish them.

Most children learned the things they needed to know at home. The history of their people was taught by their family and **griots**. The laws of their society and practical skills were taught by family, too. Education focused on the skills they needed to survive, raise children, and take their place within their community. Children participated in the chores and learned the crafts of their elders. For the **Mandinka** people who ruled Mali, children were trained by their mothers. When boys reached twelve they began to learn the occupations of their uncles.

Both boys and girls were taught how to make pottery, like this bowl, by their family.

Formal education

Sometimes boys were sent to study in the cities of Niani, Gao, or Timbuktu. There they

Boys today still learn an occupation from their uncles. In ancient times, boys were sometimes able to study in Timbuktu.

would study a subject or profession with a master scholar. Sankore University in Timbuktu was a center of learning. The influence of **Islam** and a desire to read the **Qur'an** brought about increased interest in reading and writing throughout ancient West Africa.

How do we know?

Archaeologists have found toys shaped like animals at Jenne. The toys reflect children's interest in animals. Many manuscripts have been found at Timbuktu that have helped preserve the history of learning in West Africa.

This is one of the many manuscripts found at Timbuktu. The text is written in **Arabic,** the primary language of **Muslims.**

Religion and Sacred Places

Religion

West Africa has shaped itself within the traditions of native religions and **Islam**. A variety of native beliefs focus on spirits. Animals were often considered gods. Traditional religions varied depending on whether they worshiped one god or many. Some religions had special priests, and others were led by rulers.

The Soninke wore charms like these for protection from spirits that they thought might harm them.

The Soninke people of Ghana celebrated their religion in rituals, song, dance, and prayers. They believed in a single Creator and that everything living and nonliving had a spirit. They believed that spirits could do good or evil to them. The Songhai people used cone-shaped earthen or stone pillars to mark places where they believed an ancestor's spirit resided.

Ghana was conquered by a group of Muslims called the Almoravids. They were led by Ibn Yasin. The religious community that he formed was called a ribat. His followers became known as al-Murabitun, "the people of the ribat."

Islam

Islam was a big influence in West Africa. **Muslims** believe in one all-powerful and merciful God. They believe that God's word was handed to them by the prophet Muhammed. As Muslims from other regions visited West Africa, they brought goods to **trade** as well as new ideas. Many West Africans were converted to Islam.

Sacred places

Several **mosques** from ancient West African times are still standing. West Africans built their mosques out of dried earth and decorated them with wooden projections and patterns in the clay. Almost all mosques had a minaret. A minaret was a high tower from which Muslims were called to daily prayer. In native religion, West Africans found many places and objects in the natural world to be sacred. The baobab tree is still believed by some West Africans to hold powerful spirits. The tree may even be guarded by a villager.

In West Africa, mosques mix Islamic style with native religion. For example, the minaret was designed to resemble the ancestor markers of the Songhai.

Medicine and Healing

Ancient West Africa was a place were a variety of parasites and diseases flourished. **Malaria** was one of the most common and deadliest diseases. It was found in all but the coolest and driest regions, where mosquitoes could not live. The tsetse fly spread **sleeping sickness,** another serious illness.

The **Sahara** provided a natural barrier to some of the diseases that afflicted other regions. Also, many diseases and parasites that would prove deadly to travelers had a milder effect on Africans. This is because Africans had developed resistance to some diseases over the centuries.

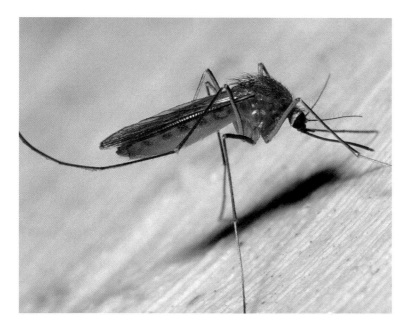

The mosquito was one of the most dangerous insects in Africa because it spread malaria.

Objects like this may have been used to perform surgeries in the ancient city of Jenne.

Healing

Common healing methods included spiritual healing, where spirits were sought for a cure. Folk medicine was also widely known and practiced.

The ancient city of Jenne was known as a medical center. Cataract eye surgery was performed there. Women received medical advice about childbearing. Also, in Jenne during ancient times, the mosquito was discovered to be the cause of malaria.

Timbuktu

The city of Timbuktu was named for a woman who guarded the small **nomadic** settlement. Eventually the settlement became a great city because of its location near an **oasis.** Timbuktu soon became a meeting place for **trade** and learning.

People from both North and West Africa lived in Timbuktu. **Islam** was the main religion of the city. During the mid sixteenth century, the population reached 60,000.

The people of Timbuktu read many books. Books were valued as much as salt. Salt was difficult to obtain and so was as valuable as gold in trade. Thus books, salt, and gold were all precious to ancient West Africans.

Timbuktu was a meeting place. People traded goods and exchanged ideas there.

Timbuktu was sought by many who had heard of its splendor. The city, though, was difficult to reach for those not prepared for the climate, insects, and other hazards.

The city of Timbuktu overflowed with many scientific and technological advances. The people of Timbuktu practiced town planning and architecture. They also had a strong group of business people—many of whom had studied at schools in Timbuktu.

Books were important to the people who lived in Timbuktu. Some people had personal libraries of more than 15,000 books.

A West African Home

West African homes were built with materials from the land. They generally had circular walls of clay and cone-shaped thatched roofs. In the driest regions, roofs could be flat and made of clay with a gutter system to shed the occasional light rainfall. **Nomads** had portable, tentlike structures. Visitors from the north had homes too, built of stone in a square shape with yellow plaster interiors.

Typical houses had very few furnishings or personal belongings. Most activities happened outside. There were usually one sleeping mat or cot per person, rugs, and sometimes stools. Wooden or woven storage chests were also used in homes.

The traditional West African home was built of mud with a thatched roof that could stand up to rain.

A blend of styles

By the thirteenth and fourteenth centuries, West African architecture was a blend of styles. **Mansa** Musa introduced brick homes with flat roofs to Mali after his **pilgrimage** to **Mecca.** West Africans began to imitate the architecture of the Holy Land, even without stone or timber. They often made mud blocks and used short wooden branches gathered from the land. In **Muslim** neighborhoods, houses were rectangular and made of stone with two stories. Some had as many as nine rooms. Typically, the first floor was used for storing goods and the top floor was where the family lived.

In Muslim neighborhoods the houses were usually built of stone.

New ideas about architecture caused West Africans to experiment with building styles.

Cooking and Eating

Food

West Africans ate yams, plantains, and other vegetables and fruits. Fish and occasionally meat were eaten as well. Monkey bread—pods that contain seeds—was gathered from baobab trees. Grains and seeds of wild grasses were a main part of the West African diet.

Men and boys **cultivated** the land and planted the crops. In addition, men and boys also caught fish and hunted. Women and girls did the weeding and tended vegetables. At harvest, everyone joined in the work.

The men of this village in Mali work together to prepare freshly harvested grain, just as the ancient West Africans did.

Girls learned how to make pottery from their mothers. Pots were used to carry water and food. Meat and fish were dried in special perforated pots. Gourds and pottery were often used for bowls.

In West Africa, rich families enjoyed more variety in their diet than other families. The rich would eat beef, mutton, or chicken more often. In Ghana, visitors were always welcome to share a meal. A family would usually offer visitors green peppers stuffed with rice, milk, fruit, and meat.

This girl probably helped to make the pottery that she is using to transport food. With this pottery, she is able to carry an entire meal on her head.

In West Africa today, women and girls usually weed and tend the vegetable gardens just like in ancient times.

Games

Chess, dancing, fencing, gymnastics, and poetry reading were enjoyed by West Africans. **Cowrie** shells and seeds were used to play games like jacks. Mancala, thought to be the oldest game in the world, was created in Africa. Pieces are moved around a board and captured by each player. It was played in the dirt with pebbles by most people and on ivory boards decorated with gold by rich people. Tic-tac-toe and hopscotch were invented in Africa, too.

Mancala is played everywhere in Africa. These men are using the ground as their playing board, just like many ancient West Africans did.

Sports

Sports were often used to develop the strength of a warrior. Women did not participate in these types of sports.

Some activities that are considered sport in certain **cultures,** such as fishing and hunting, were not considered sport in ancient West Africa. These things were necessary for survival and were taken very seriously. They were not considered entertainment. Sometimes it was difficult for outsiders to tell whether an activity was for fun. Many things that would look like fun and games to some people were important **rites of initiation** for young West Africans.

Sports were often meant as practice for being a warrior. These young men are wrestling for a crowd of spectators.

Griots

A **griot** is a storyteller, but also a keeper of history and an adviser. Griots pass traditions and other important information from generation to generation. Music plays a part in their storytelling. Instruments, such as drums, may accompany the griot as they tell a story.

Everyone could tell stories, but griots served a special role in the community. Griots were able to remember large amounts of history and tradition. It was their job to hold on to as much information as they could.

Ouagadou-Bida

One traditional West African story is of *Ouagadou-Bida: The Sacred Serpent.* It tells of Ghana and how health, happiness, and peace were granted by the spirit serpent named Ouagadou-Bida. To please the spirit serpent a beautiful woman was chosen to be sacrificed to him. A warrior named Amadou Sefedokote battled the serpent and stole his bride. He and the woman galloped away on a horse, never to be seen again. After this happened, the kingdom of Ghana suffered a season of drought—punishment for what Amadou Sefedokote had done.

Musicians would sometimes assist a griot as a story is told.

Music

Many musical instruments were made with simple materials. The hollowed-out dried shells of gourds became amplifiers in instruments such as the **balaphon.** Drums were made of wood and covered with animal skins. Drums were important elements of ceremony, **trade,** storytelling, and celebration. Small, handheld thumb pianos were made by attaching metal or wooden strips to a sounding board.

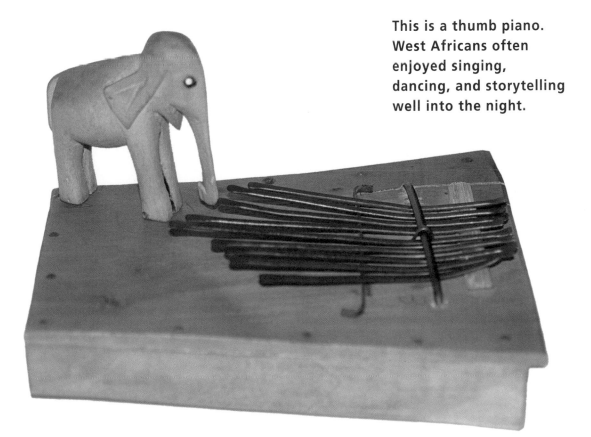

This is a thumb piano. West Africans often enjoyed singing, dancing, and storytelling well into the night.

Crafts and Craftworkers

Creativity was viewed as a gift from god. West Africans used art to express their beliefs and views of the world. Paintings shared stories. Masks were created for ceremonies. The ancient West African style of art has influenced modern art around the world today.

Blacksmiths

Blacksmiths were especially honored by West Africans. Their ability to shape tools from metal ore was considered to be magical. Their skills were passed from generation to generation.

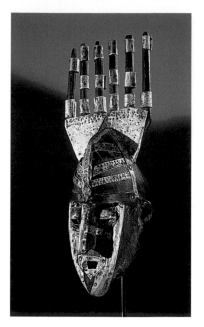

Masks were often used for special ceremonies.

Blacksmiths were considered magicians by many ancient West Africans because they could control metal and fire.

Weaving

West Africans believed that a spider was sent by the gods to teach people his magic of weaving. Each part of a loom had meaning. Before weaving, the weaver touched the loom and said a prayer. The loom then was believed to sing a song that only the weaver could hear while weaving.

Other crafts practiced in ancient West Africa were pottery making, jewelry making, carving, and sandal making. Since men did the hunting and farming, they made bows, arrows, spears, hoes, and axes. Baskets, pots, and utensils were made by both men and women.

This woman is weaving cloth on a loom similar to that used by ancient West Africans.

Work and Workers

In the kingdoms of ancient West Africa, work and home life were closely related. West Africans worked in a variety of occupations, from **griot** to teacher to farmer.

In the country

In the country, farming and raising livestock were common occupations. A portion of the food or goods produced were used by the family. The extra food or goods were **traded** for things they wanted. People who lived along waterways were usually fishers and boat builders.

Where a person lived usually determined what type of work they did. This man lives in the country and is a farmer.

In the cities of ancient West Africa, market scenes like this were common. People who lived in the cities had various occupations. Some were lawyers, scientists, writers, and teachers.

In the city

In urban areas people made crafts. Weavers, blacksmiths, and other craftworkers created useful and beautiful goods. Other professions were created to go along with the advances in law, education, military service, sciences, and trade. Some professions were determined by gender and some were determined by **clans.**

People in the country and city areas relied on each other. Those in the cities needed food from the rural farmers. The rural farmers got their crafts and other goods from the people living in the cities.

West African Merchants

Not all the **merchants** of West Africa were from West Africa. Merchants from the Middle East traveled to West Africa and set up areas in the towns for their homes and shops.

Money

Goods were often **traded** for other goods without a need for money. **Traders** sometimes used **cowrie** shells as money. The cowrie shell provided a uniform currency that could be accepted by merchants, traders, and farmers from various places.

Small chunks of salt were sometimes used as money, too. At times, salt was so craved by the ancient West Africans, that it was traded pound for pound for gold.

Cowrie shells were sometimes used as money by West Africans.

Gold dust was also used to pay for goods. Gold nuggets were regulated by the king of Ghana. The king wanted to control the economy and prevent a decrease in gold's value. A decrease in value would occur if its supply was too abundant.

The gold **dinar** eventually replaced the cowrie shell as the common unit for trade in West Africa. The **Muslim** sultans in Morocco, Tunisia, and Egypt made dinars with gold that was traded to them from Ghana.

These gold earrings might have been traded for salt or another good that a West African desired.

51

Canoes

Where a person lived determined what type of transportation they used. The rivers provided one way to travel from place to place. West Africans made dugout canoes from fallen trees.

On the upper reaches of the Niger River, where large trees were scarce, canoes were made from two smaller trees stitched together with cord.

Today, the people of West Africa still use dugout canoes, similar to those from ancient times, for water travel.

Camels

The desert created a need for transportation that could withstand heat and the lack of water. The camel is well adapted to the desert. People traveled on them and used them to carry goods across the desert. The camel may be the hardiest animal on Earth. A camel can drink over 26 gallons (100 liters) of water at a time, then go without water for up to nine days. Camels can tolerate heat without perspiring. Their kidneys are able to flush wastes from their bodies without using much water. Camels can fill up on food when it's available, then go without eating for a long time. They can live off of their excess stored fat without losing muscle. They can also carry more than 330 pounds (150 kilograms).

The camel is the perfect animal for desert travel. It can carry heavy loads and go for many days without eating or drinking.

Other methods

Carts were impractical in the desert as the wheels easily got stuck in the sand. Donkeys were sometimes used to carry goods. People often carried items in regions where tsetse flies and a lack of pasture prevented the use of pack animals.

Trade and Trade Routes

The kingdoms of Ghana, Mali, and Songhai all have a thriving history of **trade.** Even before visitors traveled across the **Sahara** to trade, West Africans had traded among themselves for a long time.

Caravans with 12,000 or more camels carried such things as wheat, sugar, fruit, salt, and cloth through West Africa. These items were exchanged for gold and other goods.

Salt

Salt was especially prized in West Africa since it was used to flavor and preserve foods. The most plentiful salt was in the Sahara where it was naturally left in great slabs. Workers would mine the salt found there.

West Africans often craved salt because of their dry, hot climate. Today, they still trade it in great slabs.

Slaves

Slaves were often captives of war, but they could sometimes work their way out of slavery. Slaves were trained as bodyguards, soldiers, or household workers. Many worked as salt or metal miners, on plantations, or on building projects. There were many laws governing the treatment of slaves. They were often regarded as members of a household. Some slaves were educated and even became governors or advisers to their rulers. Some slaves, however, were treated harshly.

Most of the trade in West Africa during this time period was within West Africa or North Africa and **Arab** regions. There was also contact with Europe by way of the sea by 1472.

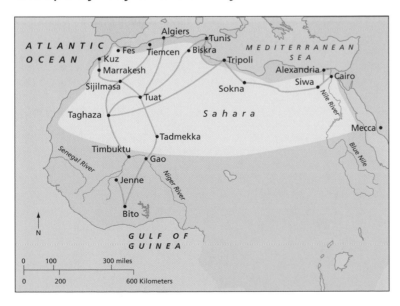

Gold

The gold of Ghana was mined by the people of Wangara. They lived in the savanna south of the kingdom of Ghana. They kept the exact location of their mines a secret. To trade, the Wangara brought their gold to a trading **site. Merchants** laid out their goods and beat drums to announce the start of trade. The Wangara, who had remained out of sight, emerged only after the merchants departed. They placed an amount of gold for trade next to the goods. Then the Wangara retreated and waited for the merchants to return and either accept the gold in exchange or retreat and wait for a better offer.

This map shows the trade routes that the ancient West Africans used when transporting goods throughout the region.

Weapons and Warfare

During much of ancient West Africa's history, there was relatively little warfare. Generally, most struggles occurred when one empire grew weak and another rose to take its place. Travelers who visited West Africa often wrote about how peaceful the streets and people were. The kingdoms of West Africa found that **trade** gave them more power than fighting a war could.

Weapons

Though gold and salt made Ghana rich, iron made them strong. Iron ore was plentiful in the Sudan. It was easier to obtain then other metals, such as copper or bronze. Tools made of iron were stronger, sharper, and more durable than those made of wood, copper, stone, bone, or bronze. Their weapons were usually spears. Strong weapons were a main factor in Ghana's rise to kingdom.

The Songhai kingdom was built on military strength as well. A full-time army and navy gave Songhai great military influence over the rest of West Africa. If a conflict arose, they were ready. Another advance in

In the rise and fall of kingdoms, much depended on military strength. For Ghana, iron weapons made them strong. For the Songhai, a new weapon, the **harquebus**, brought downfall. This man carries a harquebus over his shoulder.

weapons, however, brought the downfall of the Songhai empire. The harquebus, an early version of a gun, gave an advancing Moroccan army the advantage when they battled Songhai for its empire.

Ancient West Africans wore special clothing to protect them in battle. This man wears a type of armor and helmet and carries a spear and shield.

The decline of the West African kingdoms was caused by many factors. Internal disputes, disease, climate changes, and changes in **trade** caused kingdoms to weaken. When the Songhai kingdom fell to the Moroccans, chaos erupted in West Africa. **Traders** no longer wanted to travel there for fear of violence awaiting them. Also, traders began to travel along a coastal route, thus no longer needing to travel inland through West Africa. European involvement in the slave trade and colonization furthered the decline of the West African kingdoms.

A war with the Almoravids brought the fall of Ghana. Internal struggles and the rise of Gao brought the downfall of Mali. Invasion

Artifacts, like these pieces of pottery, are windows into the past when the kingdoms of West Africa flourished.

and the invention of the **harquebus** by Moroccans ended the Songhai kingdom. The great kingdoms of Ghana, Mali, and Songhai rose and fell while most of the world did not realize that these **cultures** even existed.

Despite these setbacks, many traditional West African family values and religious beliefs have remained intact. The people of West Africa have a heritage of intellect, spirituality, creative expression, and diplomacy. Their strong oral tradition and family values influenced not only the kingdoms of West Africa, but also every culture that had contact with the area.

There is still art, literature, and other human gifts that have brought attention to the cultures of West Africa. Artists such as Pablo Picasso were influenced by African art. Traditional African drumming can be heard performed in many countries outside Africa.

The history of West Africa has revealed remarkable and advanced civilizations. Africa, once unknown to outsiders, has captivated the human imagination as new discoveries constantly reveal a history even more compelling than imagined.

The traditions of West Africa remain alive through art. Many art styles seen in West Africa today have been influenced by ancient times.

Time Line

B.C.E.

c. 1000   **Trade** between farming communities in West Africa began.

c. 300   The Iron Age began.

C.E.

c. 300–500   The empire of Ghana began to emerge.

c. 300–99   The camel is introduced to Africa, making it easier to travel across the **Sahara.**

c. 700   The Soninke people are unified by a warrior and **diplomat** from the Ouagadou **clan.**

1076   The Almoravids, a group of **Muslims,** defeated Ghana. The kingdom of Mali emerged.

c. 1235   Sundiata Keita defeated Sumanguru and became known as the Lion King.

1312–37   **Mansa** Musa ruled Mali.

1324   Mansa Musa made his **pilgrimage** to **Mecca.**

1325   Mansa Musa captured the city of Gao.

1337–60   Mansa Suleyman ruled Mali. The kingdom of Songhai emerged.

1464   **Sunni** Ali became king of Songhai.

1473   Siege of Jenne by Sunni Ali.

1493   **Askia** Muhammed came to power.

1591   Songhai overthrown by Moroccan army.

Other West African Cultures

Ghana, Mali, and Songhai were the largest and best known kingdoms of ancient West Africa. There were, however, other important civilizations in West Africa as well.

The Nok civilization lasted from about 1000 B.C.E.–600 C.E. They lived in the area that we now call Nigeria. Not much is known about them, but terra-cotta figurines have been discovered by **archaeologists.** The figurines are interesting representations that show great imagination. Some of the figurines are life-size.

Later, in the same region, Yoruba people built their civilization. Their art was seen in 1911 by a German named Leo Frobenius. He discovered that old pieces of artwork were dug up by the Yoruba for religious ceremonies and then returned to the earth. Not knowing that Africa had produced great civilizations, he thought he had discovered the lost city of Atlantis. The Ife **culture** of West Africa was the real source of the **artifacts** he found. According to Yoruba legend, Ife is where the gods came down and populated the earth. It is also said that the Yoruba taught metal casting to the people of Benin.

The people of Benin, another Yoruba rain forest kingdom, were in contact with travelers from Portugal by the mid 1400s. Like the Nok and Ife, they demonstrated a very sophisticated culture through their art and crafts.

While none of these kingdoms attained the political power or vast territory of Ghana, Mali, or Songhai, they were advanced civilizations with traditions that have been carried into modern West Africa.

Glossary

Arab person born or living in the Arabian Peninsula; a member of a people that speak Arabic

archaeologist person who learns about life in the past by looking for and studying objects from earlier times

artifact object made by people

Askia Songhai military rank, later used as a title for ruler

balaphon musical instrument, similar to a xylophone, that uses dried gourds to provide amplification

clan group of people with a common ancestor

coup rapid military or political takeover

cowrie type of shell sometimes used as money by ancient West Africans

cultivate to prepare land for the raising of crops

culture way of life

dialect form of a language belonging to a certain region

dinar gold coin

diplomat person who works to keep good relations between governments of different countries

excavate to carefully dig up buried objects to find out about the past

exile to leave one's country either by force or for safety

fertile ability to have children; or the ability to grow plants

ghana "war chief" in the Mande language

griot person who acts as a storyteller and keeper of West African history and traditions

harquebus early form of a gun

Islam religion based on belief in Allah as the only God, in Muhammed as his prophet, and in the Qur'an

jihad Muslim "holy war"

liberate to set free

malaria serious disease that is spread by the bite of one kind of mosquito

Mandinka people who founded the kingdom of Mali

mansa "lord" in the Mandinka language

Mecca birthplace of Muhammed and Muslim holy city. Muslims believe that they should travel to Mecca at least once during their lifetimes.

merchant person who buys and sells goods

mosque Muslim place of worship

Muslim person whose religion is Islam

nomad member of a people who have no fixed home, but wander from place to place

oasis fertile or green spot in the desert

official member of a government or clan who has certain authoritative duties

pilgrimage journey to a holy place, often as an act of devotion

primate biological grouping of mammals that includes humans, apes, and monkeys

qadi Muslim judge

Qur'an Muslim holy book

ruin remains of something destroyed

rite of initiation traditional ceremony or event that marks the passage from childhood to adulthood

Sahara largest desert in the world, filling nearly all of northern Africa. The Sahara has a total area of 3,320,000 square miles (8,600,000 square kilometers).

site place where something is found or took place

sleeping sickness serious illness spread by tsetse flies

Sunni "king;" name given to ruler of Songhai kingdom

terra incognita phrase meaning "unknown land," often applied to Africa because it was difficult to travel to

trade to buy and sell goods

trader person who makes a living by buying and selling goods

More Books to Read

Brooks, Larry. *Daily Life in Ancient & Modern Timbuktu.* Minneapolis: Runestone Press, 1999.

MacDonald, Fiona. *An Ancient African Town.* Danbury, Conn.: Franklin Watts, 1998.

Nelson, Julie. *West African Kingdoms.* Austin, Tex.: Raintree Steck-Vaughn, 2001.

Index